Let Me Go
So I Can Grow

PASTOR DENISE L. WADE

WESTBOW·
PRESS
A DIVISION OF THOMAS NELSON
& ZONDERVAN

Scripture taken from the King James Version of the Bible.

Scripture taken from the New King James Version. Copyright © 1979, 1980, 1982 by Thomas Nelson, Inc. Used by permission. All rights reserved.

Scripture taken from the Holy Bible, NEW INTERNATIONAL VERSION®. Copyright © 1973, 1978, 1984, 2011 by Biblica, Inc. All rights reserved worldwide. Used by permission. NEW INTERNATIONAL VERSION® and NIV® are registered trademarks of Biblica, Inc. Use of either trademark for the offering of goods or services requires the prior written consent of Biblica US, Inc.

Scripture quotations taken from the Holy Bible, New Living Translation, Copyright © 1996, 2004. Used by permission of Tyndale House Publishers, Inc., Wheaton, Illinois 60189. All rights reserved.

NET Bible® copyright ©1996-2006 by Biblical Studies Press, L.L.C. http://netbible.com All rights reserved.

Scripture taken from the Amplified Bible, copyright © 1954, 1958, 1962, 1964, 1965, 1987 by The Lockman Foundation. Used by permission.

WestBow Press books may be ordered through booksellers or by contacting:

WestBow Press
A Division of Thomas Nelson & Zondervan
1663 Liberty Drive
Bloomington, IN 47403
www.westbowpress.com
1 (866) 928-1240

ISBN: 978-1-4908-6525-6 (sc)

Library of Congress Control Number: 2015900078

Print information available on the last page.

WestBow Press rev. date: 10/28/2015

EXPRESSIONS OF ENDEARMENT

I would first like to thank Jesus Christ who is my Lord and Savior for giving me the strength, the will, the wisdom and knowledge to write this book. I give you all honor and glory. I thank God for Apostle Kogie Porter who has been a blessing to my life. Thank you for your teaching, encouragement and prayers. I bless God for my children Dayana and Zani, my grandchildren Zamarion and Zyaire with lots of love, hugs and kisses. To my sisters and brothers in Christ thank you for your prayers and encouragement. To my family, I love you and bless God for each of you. Again I give Jesus Christ all the glory.

INTRODUCTION

I bless God for this opportunity. It is a privilege and honor to write this book to help those that have been hurt through ministry. This book is written to open the eyes of God's people to satan's tricks and to get ministers, christians and ministries back to work, back to a household of faith, back to worshiping the Lord and back to doing what God called you to do. I pray that every reader would receive deliverance, conviction, healing, wisdom and knowledge. I am not telling anyone to leave the ministry that they are in; my situation may not be as yours. You have to seek God first in all things. He will lead you, guide you and direct you. If this book, changes one life, than my pain was not in vain. All honor and glory will be to the Lord. Amen.

CONTENTS

CHAPTER 1 – THE SET UP

All confusion began to break loose in my life. I was surrounded by people that I thought cared for me and my children. When you are in a storm, you get to see who is for you and who is against you. I felt like I was in a place where I just wanted to sleep and wake up when the storm was all over. There was nowhere for me to turn. Friends were not friends, family could not help me. I remembered that the pain hurt so bad I began to cry out to God. Just a few months prior to this situation, I ran in to an old friend who was on her way to church. As I was crying out to God, He reminded me of our meeting. I called my friend with my eyes filled with tears and asked for the address of her church. God began to minister to me and He began to show me all the times when He was trying to get my attention, and I ignored Him. This time, God had to put the fire up seven times greater. He now has my undivided attention.

The first day I walked in the church it was a wonderful service and the message was for me. I remember crying so much that after service, someone came to me and said pastor would like to see you. I went in her office and she said to me you are going to be blessed. I told her what was happening in my life and she assured me that God will work everything out. I felt so comfortable, my children and I attended two more services and I knew that I was home. I joined the ministry. I was so excited about the ministry. I kept going to church hearing the word of God and it seemed as though things were getting worse in my life. The statement things will get worse before they get better was so real. Here I was a single mother of two going through and I tried everything else I thought, why not try God. He was the only one that could help me get out of the mess. I began to get closer and closer to God. My pastor helped me through this difficult experience in my life. God knew what he was doing by connecting me to such a wonderful pastor as this, she continued to encourage me, minister to me and was there for me through it all. My children loved her and so did I.

When you give your life to Christ, He begins to show you, and He will take off the blinders on your eyes so that you can see others. I began to see where I went wrong as a parent and understanding why I was going through this now. I just knew that I was in the right place now getting to know God and His word. My life was really changing. God will set you up so good that your bad situation becomes a journey to your destiny. I was switching jobs at this time, a nurse aide to a correction officer. I remember being in the academy for seven weeks, I could only come home on the weekend. It was very difficult for me to leave my children during this time, but I wanted a better life for them so, I did what I had to do. While in the academy this helped to discipline me and I learned so much. As I look back I do not know how I got through the academy although, I was there physically, but my mind was on all that I was going through. I can only say it was God that got me through.

Every Sunday I would go to church and leave from church to the academy this helped me get through the week until next Sunday. It was a few obstacles in my way but I made it. God set me up with great friends in the academy that wanted me to succeed. We were like a family. It was now time to start my new position. I was missing out on church because I was not off on Sunday's. Whenever I was off on Sunday, I was in church. I continued to stay in communication with my pastor and I stayed prayerful with God. I remember my pastor told me that God was sending me to work in this position and that many are going to share their personal life with me. This was so true co-workers began to share with me all that was was going on in their life. This was another set up God began to let me see that my situation is not that bad.

I remember a co-worker had to go to court and I felt that I should go with her. I told my pastor that I feel like going with her and my pastor said than you should go. This was another set up I was having a heart of compassion and not thinking about myself but wanting to help another. I found that the more I was there to help others, God began to move in my situations, I got to know Him even the more. I was ministering and praying for many. I felt good like this is why I am here. I now see my purpose in life. I realized that I needed God all along. It was by His grace and His mercy that I made it this far without Him. He was now the head of my life. Who better to trust, God knows what is best for me. He began to set me up with new friends as He stripped me from the old friends. There was only a handful of old friends left these are the true and real friends. Go through something in your life and you will see who will whether the storm with you. My life was finally going in the right direction things where starting to get better. Prayer changes things. I now have a new family in ministry and the pain slowly changed to joy. I tried to make peace with some and those that did not receive it, I kept it moving. As much as I tried to fight to keep those relationships, God was pulling me out of them. I began to understand it by and by.

While I continued to hear the word of God, I was changing so fast. I no longer had a desire to live like I used to. I was getting delivered and convicted all at once. After the storm came peace, joy and happiness. I love God even more. The set up was that God had me in a place right where He wanted me so, that He can change my whole life around. He heard my cry and felt my pain. God began to put my life that was so out of order in order. I am finally growing and becoming wiser as I am getting to know God more and more. My faith was growing by hearing the word of God and seeing God move in my life.

I was now three and a half years into ministry and everything was great. My pastor saw the growth in me and God moving in my life. I give all honor and glory to Jesus Christ. We will often find ourselves, being in a place where no one can help us, no one can save us, and no one can fix our situation but God. We cannot call our mother, father, not a friend, your pastor can help encourage you, minister the word of God to you and help lead you to having your own personal relationship with God. There is an old saying you have to try Him for yourself. Well I am trying Him and He is wonderful, He is good and awesome the way He continues to show up and fix things. I know He loves me.

At this point of my spiritual journey, I began to go through changes. I could be walking and I would feel a strong wind. This was God blowing His ruah (breath) in me. I would be sleeping and get awoken by the Holy Spirit in the middle of the night and this was going on for a little while and I finally shared this with my pastor. My pastor said God is calling you. When she spoke those words, I began to get a quickening in me and I remember saying what does that mean, she said God is calling you to ministry. This was beginning to make sense on what I was feeling and as time went on I was called minister. My pastor saw the compassion in me and how I would run to the aide of others. It was determined that I had a heart of a pastor. This was the call on my life. I began to feel the struggles of the people and finding that my situation is not that bad and all that I had to go through was for this moment here. My pastor shared with me the vision that God gave her for the ministry. There would be six cities where a church would be planted under her Apostolic leadership and she would oversee and God would raise up pastors. There were three other pastors that were being raised up. One would take over my pastors ministry. I would open a church in the next city and there were two more pastors that God raised up to take over two more cities, and there would be four churches.

I began my spiritual journey as a minister of religious education. I enrolled in theological school which my pastor opened this campus in her church. Here is where I received my Diploma in theology, associate in theology, bachelor in theology, master of divinity and Dr. of ministry. Praise God this was all God's doing, He was continuing to set me up. Now came the time to open my church and my pastor went with me to the city God was sending me to. I asked the Director of the program if I can rent space in the facilities and the answer was yes he asked me when would you like to start I said February 1, 2004. Yes five years into ministry and it was now time for me to be in my rightful position in ministry. The third city opened up on the same day and the fourth opened in April. I was so excited I remember advertising and putting out flyer's for the gathering. Eight people showed up and they all joined the ministry praise the Lord.

I began to grow as a pastor. I continued to call my pastor for wise counsel and there were times she would show up and surprise me and I would be very nervous. It is very hard to have your chatechizer, (teacher of religious education) your pastor in front of you unexpected it appeared to be that she was there to critique me which was hard. My ministry was beginning to grow and God raised the first evangelist and prophet. I began to minister to them and work with them over the phone. My pastor suggested that she would train my ministers. God was moving in my life and my ministry. This was my purpose from the time I was in my mother's womb. My pastor suggested that my church and the third church would come together, one Sunday out of the month. The fourth church was too far away to come. We thought this was a good idea so we did. I began to look back on my spiritual journey and realize that all that I had to go through was to get me to this place and I thank God for my experiences, my trials and tribulations. It made me stronger, my faith grew, and how can I minister to others if I did not go through. So my set back became my set up.

A MESSAGE TO YOU- THE SET UP-ARRANGED
TO RESULT IN AN EASY VICTORY.

Our setbacks are often our setups. I realized in my walk with Jesus, whenever all turmoil seemed to break loose around me soon after I received a blessing from the Lord. Satan likes to come and distract you from the blessing that is coming your way. God promises that if we do not become tired of doing what is good,we will reap a harvest of blessings. So let's not get tired of doing what is good. At just the right time we will reap a harvest of blessings if we don't give up. (Galatians 6:9 NLT) Do not give up things are about to get better. Watch God. We must continue to be strong and immovable. So, my dear brothers and sisters, be strong and immovable. "Always work enthusiastically for the Lord, for nothing you do for the Lord is ever useless." (1 Corinthians 15:58 NLT) Always work enthusiastically for the Lord for you know that nothing you do is ever useless. Continue to stand in the mist of adversity and you will receive victory and all the honor and glory will belong to Jesus Christ. Embrace what God is doing in your life. He is setting you up for greater things. I pray and I thank God for the strength that He will give you in our weakness and in the insults, hardships, persecutions and troubles that we suffer for Christ. "That's why I take pleasure in my weaknesses, and in the insults, hardships, persecutions, and troubles that I suffer for Christ. For when I am weak, then I am strong." (2 Corinthians 12:10 NLT). "I can do all things through Christ which strengthens me." (Philipians 4:13 KJV). I pray that each and every reader will see God like you have never seen Him before. God will move mightily in your life and in your situation if you allow Him to. He will remove every hindrance out of your life. Let God in and let Him have His way in your life. Trust Him. "Be strong and of good courage, do not fear nor be afraid of them; for the Lord your God, He is the One who goes with you. He will not leave you nor forsake you." (Deuteronomy 31:6 NKJV). When you are going through now is not the time to give up, if you are faithful to God, He will be faithful to you. There are blessings with your name on it and no one can take them from you. When you find yourself in the place where people around you say to you,you have changed consider this a wonderful thing that God is doing a new thing in you. "For I am about to do something new. See, I have already begun! Do you not see it? I will make a pathway through the wilderness. I will create rivers in the dry wasteland." (Isaiah 43:19 NLT). **Stay focused on Jesus Christ and you will receive all that He has destined for you.**

CHAPTER 2 – A HEART OF COMPASSION

I was getting to know the sheep in my congregation. As their pastor, I was there when the sheep needed me as they faced difficult situations. I began to get too close to my congregation. I remember my pastor shared that pastors are to be friends with everyone, but have no friends. I understand that statement by and by. Sometimes pastors can get too close to the sheep and you have to know when it is too much. I began to love the congregation too much and I did not always feel that love back. I cried many nights because sheep bite and it hurts. As pastors, we do not have the right to bite back.

As a pastor, I was going through so much in my personal life but you would not know it unless I told you. I knew that it was not about me, it was about others. I have learned how to give things over to God. I experienced many disappointments, this kept me humble, gave me strength that I did not realize I had, kept pride from rising up, and caused my faith to grow even more. My heart was filled with compassion. No longer did I focus on my situation, I was busy helping others. All that I had to go through; all the trials and tribulations became my ministry. God began to birth a healing ministry within my church, and to help build up the brokenhearted and help in the process of becoming whole through Jesus Christ. My ministry theme became (Isaiah 61:1-3 NLT). "The Spirit of the Sovereign Lord is upon me, for the Lord has anointed me to bring good news to the poor. He has sent me to comfort the brokenhearted and to proclaim that captives will be released and prisoners will be freed. He has sent me to tell those who mourn that the time of the Lord's favor has come, and with it the day of God's anger against their enemies. To all who mourn in Israel, He will give a crown of beauty for ashes, a joyous blessing instead of mourning, festive praise instead of despair. In their righteousness, they will be like great oaks that the Lord has planted for His own glory." This is the air that I breathe to help those that are brokenhearted. I understood by and by why? I had to go through so many heartbreaking experiences and why? I had to cry many nights. How can I preach the good news of Jesus Christ with such conviction if I have never experienced hardship in my life?

I ministered to the hearts of the people, helped to build them up with encouragement and counseled when needed. Their healing became my healing. The more I ministered to people God healed me. I give God all the praise and honor. One thing is for sure I want to always remain humble and I thank God for my humble spirit. My faith continued to grow God was giving me a bold spirit and I really began to walk by faith and not by sight. I did not care what things appeared to be I just knew that Jesus Christ was on my side and He showed up before, He will show up again. I began to really see that no weapons formed against me shall prosper.

For everything there is a season and a reason. With each level that God takes you to there is an awakening and there is awareness. Pastors are constantly changing because God continues to do a work in them and in order to get to the next level we have to first past the test in each level to get to the next. This is where that old saying comes in I may not be where I want to be but I am sure not where I used to be. I thank God from where He has brought me from, and I could not have gotten this far without Him. I need Him every step of the way. We cannot do anything without God. We are nothing without Him. If we truly let God lead us, guide us and direct us; watch God show up in your life and make a difference in your life. When God directs us, everything begins to work out for His good purpose in our lives. He loves us so much and He wants the best for us. God continues to bless my life and I have been delivered and convicted from so many things.

Every pastor needs a vacation. I have gone on vacation twice. I went on a cruise and to Florida and both were with the church. I have not gone on a trip with my family. It had a lot to do with the demands from my leader. I was too intimidated to say I need to go on a vacation because who is going to run my church. It was always said if you need to go away, one of the other ministers will come and fill in while you are away. It was spoken but the option was never really put into place to take advantage of the offer.

There must be a balance in the pastors life and in ministry. Even Jesus got away sometimes going up to the mountain and spending time with God. God would want us to spend time with our family. When going away, you take those moments where it is just you and God so that when you return back you are refreshed. Pastors, we have to get delivered from all work and no play. God wants us to also, have fun. I work a full-time job and I get 6 weeks of vacation time every year. Why? Because you need a break from work and I found even having that time off I can come back refreshed. Call it a retreat we need that or else ministry can put demands on you and you will carry the weight on your shoulder.

Your family sees the demands that ministry and your leader can have on you. Family wants to stay away from the God that you serve because of unrealistic demands. When family gatherings would come up, I said I am sorry I cannot make it, because I have church, or choir rehearsal or school. There has to be a balance in your life as well as ministry. If I was encouraged to take a vacation, I would have done it. I remember when I had surgery (fibroid tumors removed) and the surgery would have me to miss church for 2-3 weeks and I remember my pastor said to me "Pastor do not worry I will make sure your members get to church you should have this surgery at this time." I had the surgery with a peaceful mind. Surgery went very well and my doctor said that I should not drive for at least 3-4 weeks. I stayed in the hospital for 5 days and I remember my first day home, my pastor called me and told me off. She said "You cannot ever just leave your ministry and not make away for your members to get to church." That went through me like a knife and this was the first time in all my years of pastoring that I missed a Sunday. I cried so much my stomach hurt and I still had stitches. I never said anything to my pastor about this ever. I felt so guilty and I told my pastor that I would have a minister, drive my truck and I would be back in my church the next Sunday. She said "Are you sure pastor, I said "yes" she never talked me out of it.

The minister did drive me to church and after service I drove her to work going against my doctors instructions on not driving. This experience helped increase my heart of compassion and I remember thinking to myself I do not ever want to put such demands on my ministers ever. God is love He is not cruel and heartless. God is caring and compassionate, gentle and kind. God is concerned about us. Through it all, I kept my mind on Jesus Christ and I use to say I can see how someone would want to leave a ministry. Thank God I healed from this surgery because Jesus is the ultimate healer. This was yet another disappointment, but I kept it moving. I was too rooted, devoted and grounded in ministry leaving was never an option. I am not a quitter and will stand through many adversities, I was steadfast and immovable. We have to be extremely careful that our life situations and disappointing moments do not cause us to become bitter and angry. They are only to make you stronger and better. Through every obstacle in my life, God was filling me with a heart of compassion. Every pastor must have love for people just as Jesus does. We cannot let our emotions get in the way. If you are walking with a hardened heart, let God in to chisel it away this can happen through the word of God and through prayer. As a believer, it is highly imperative that you always stay surrounded by positive influences. It is my daily prayer that everyone would have a heart of compassion for all people as this world would be a much better place.

A MESSAGE TO YOU- A HEART OF COMPASSION-DEEP SYMPATHY, CONSIDERATION AND KINDNESS

We need a heart of compassion so that we do not become judgmental and we will be able to love others with Godly love. We can get a stony heart and a hardened heart because of anger, bitterness, and jealousy. The bible tells us that God will make us new. "I will give you a new heart and I will put a new spirit in you. I will take out your stony, stubborn heart and give you a tender responsive heart." (Ezekiel 36:26 NLT).

"I pray and thank God for replacing your stony heart with a heart of compassion so that we can love each other and help one another in the way that God wants us to.Humble yourselves before the Lord, and he will lift you up in honor." (James 4:10 NLT). God wants us to be compassionate to one another.

(Zechariah 7:9-10 NLT) This is what the Lord of Heaven's Armies says: Judge fairly and show mercy and kindness to one another. Do not opress widows, orphans, foreigners, and the poor. And do not scheme against each other. "Therefore, as God's chosen people, holy and dearly loved, clothe yourselves with compassion, kindness, humility, gentleness and patience.Bear with each other and forgive one another if any of you has a grievance against someone. Forgive as the Lord forgave you and over all these virtues put on love which binds them all together in perfect unity." (Colossians 3:12-14 NIV). The more heartbreaks and heartaches that I had to endure kept me from getting a stony heart. It helped me to have more of a heart of compassion as long as you do not let anger seep in ask God to help you to have a heart of compassion and to keep you humble. "Finally, all of you, be like- minded, be sympathetic, love one another, be compassionate and humble. Do not repay evil with evil or insult with insult. On the contrary, repay evil with blessing, because to this you were called so that you may inherit a blessing.For whoever would love life and see good days must keep their tongue from evil and their lips from deceitful speech. They must turn from evil and do good; they must seek peace and pursue it. For the eyes of the Lord are on the righteous and his ears are attentive to their prayer, but the face of the Lord is against those who do evil." (1 Peter 3:8-12 NIV).

CHAPTER 3 – THE CALL

I remember thinking that this call on my life is bigger than me and my pastor. This call and the anointing on my life has kept me through all of the ups and downs in this ministry for fourteen years. It was not my pastor that called me it was God who called me before, He created me in my mothers' womb. You see, when God calls you, you will accomplish all that He has set out for you to do. He has already made a way for what seems to be no way. He has a ram in the bush through every obstacle that you will ever face in life. You just have to remain focused on Him regardless of what is happening around you. To God be the glory. God will set you up so good that you will have many testimonies and a testimony is not for you to keep to yourself it is to, share with others so that your story can help someone else. When you have a calling on your life, the enemy will try everything to stop it. No weapons formed against you shall prosper. There were so many distractions as I continued to build my ministry. I can definitely relate to what Nehemiah went through as the enemy kept trying to stop him from building, but just like Nehemiah, I kept on building.

The end result God receives all the glory because when you are steadfast and immovable you will always overcome every attack, scheme, tactic and trick of the enemy. I did not struggle or fight when God called me into ministry, I accepted the call right away. I surrendered myself completely as a yielded and willing vessel. When you fight the calling of God over your life, the fire always gets turned up a little hotter, in other words whatever it takes for you to surrender.

You can only teach what you have been taught until you decide to educate yourself and analyze absolutely everything. Just like when you were growing up as a child, you were taught morals and values and you followed those morals and values and as you get older, you might see that you were not always taught the right things. Conviction is revealed in your life so that you will see the "error of your ways" and do better. This happens by being under the word of God. The call on your life will cause you to know that it is not about you, it is about helping to build someone else up and to encourage others. I love ministering to someone because I know that it is not me doing this it is the Holy Spirit ministering to the hearts of the people through me as His willing and yielded vessel. When we lead an individual to Christ, God just wants to use us as His vessels and all He requires of us, is to be willing and available to be of service for Him. We are all ministers of the gospel but not everyone is called to the five fold preaching ministry which holds the following titles; apostle, pastor, teacher, evangelist and prophet. You may not have any of these titles but that does not mean that you do not have a calling on your life. We are all called to do a work for the Lord. Example, look at Oprah Winfrey she has a massive calling on her life. God called her to ministry and her ministry reaches the multitudes on a daily basis. She has both touched and impacted the lives of many tremendously. Oprah is a giver and God gave her a little and she gave much.

When God sees that He can trust you with little, He will give you so much more than you can ever imagine. The show "Doctors" has a calling to reach the multitudes in the area of health. We all have a calling even if it is being that joyful person that always brings life to any environment. This individual always comes into any environment with a smile and laughter that can become so contagious to all those around them. It is highly imperative that you have to tap into your God-given gift because we all have gifts some different than others and that's what makes us all unique. What good is it to have gifts and talents and never use them? A school teacher has a ministry to many which is to teach fundamental learning skills to every student that they are blessed to encounter.

I do not believe that everyone that is in prison has committed a crime. How do we know this due to DNA there are many being released from prison today because they have been wrongfully convicted. Many are called to prison ministry to help others and encourage others. Sometimes people meet Jesus in these situations. Remember whatever it takes to get your attention, ministry is not just in the church it should be everywhere you go. A nurse has ministry in the hospital taking care of people and nursing them back to health. No matter where or what your ministry is, having a covering (a church home) is so vital to your christian walk that you can be fed the word of God and overcome by others testimonies. Being covered will cause you to grow spiritually and you can show the love of God in your ministry.

Many people are not called to preach in church but there are many that are and if God did not call them you will know that it is not their ministry gift. Whatever you love to do is usually your gift. There are some nurses that hate their job because that is not what they are called to do. Maybe it is being a beautician because they can style hair well and they love to do it. Ministry is in each and every one of us. When you get to know God intimately, you will discover your purpose in life. When you are not afraid to preach the gospel of Jesus Christ, the enemy is very angry with you and the attacks are going to come but they will never, ever prosper. Greater is He that is in me, than He that is in the world. Every obstacle and stumbling block will always increase your faith and enhance your ministry. How can you tell someone else to hold on and have faith if you have never experienced hardship, difficulty or misfortune? This never feels good when you are in this situation but it will surely feel good when you can minister to someone else going through and share your testimony with them. We must continue to keep our eye on the prize which is Jesus Christ. Some might say, I do not know what my ministry is, it is the very thing that you are passionate about and will do without hesitation.

The very thing that you are most passionate about will become the very air that you breathe and maybe your ministry has not been birthed out of you yet, but please be completely aware of the fact that there is an ordained and appointed time that you meet up with destiny. Your gifts and calling will always catch up to you.

A MESSAGE TO YOU-THE CALL-TO AWAKEN, A SUMMONS OR AN INVITATION, TO SUMMONS FOR DUTY.

"If my people, who are called by my name, will humble themselves and pray and seek my face and turn from their wicked ways, then I will hear from heaven, and I will forgive their sin and will heal their land." (2 Chronicle 7:14 NIV). "The gatekeeper opens the gate for him, and the sheep recognize his voice and come to him. He calls his own sheep by name and leads them out. After he has gathered his own flock, he walks ahead of them, and they follow him because they know his voice." (John 10:3-4 NLT). "Peter replied, Repent and be baptized, every one of you, in the name of Jesus Christ for the forgiveness of your sins. And you will receive the gift of the Holy Spirit. The promise is for you and your children and for all who are far off-for all whom the Lord our God will call."(Acts 2:38-39 NIV). "And those he predestined, he also called; those he called, he also justified; those he justified, he also glorified. What then, shall we say in response to these things? If God is for us, who can be against us?" (Romans 8:30-31 NIV).

When God calls you a minister He does not take it back don't let any situation hinder you from the work God called you to do. "For God's gifts and His call is irrevocable." (Romans 11:29 NLT). "Jude, a servant of Jesus Christ and a brother of James, To those who are loved in God the Father and kept for Jesus Christ: Mercy, peace and love be yours in abundance." (Jude1:1-2 NIV).

Pastor Denise L. Wade

Head to God's calling. If He called you to a work then you must do it, if you were in a ministry and you left for whatever situation you cannot give up, this is the time to press on even further. It is imperative that you do not forfeit your inheritance for no one. Please! Please! Please! **GET BACK TO WORK.**

Chapter 4 – Winning Souls for Christ

As a Christian and as a minister, we are to minister wherever we go. All are welcome in the body of Christ. God is not pleased with pastors who scatter His sheep in any capacity.

We continue to pray for church growth, but when we begin to get growth, we pray them out and ignore them. I am confused when people come to church they come to the right place. As pastors, it is our job to cast out demons from the individuals and to minister to the people. Jesus said greater works shall we do. That was Jesus ministry casting out demons, healing the sick, setting captives free, and preaching the gospel. When God sends pastors sheep, we determine whether or not God will send more. If you are faithful in a few things, God will give you much more. God will not send more sheep to be hurt and slaughtered. People do not always get mad and leave the church they get hurt and leave. We must be extremely careful of how we treat God's children because we are held accountable. Churches grow in number when it is a healthy and loving church.

I remember a pastor that was to take over her pastors church. She was very young in her early twenties. The young pastor made a comment to her pastor that she did not want to be a pastor. This broke her pastors' heart to where she removed this pastor publicly in church on the Lords' day, she said God is removing her and began to tell all these faults and reasons why God was removing her as she read Jeremiah 22. We were told not to cry or mourn for this pastor and that she will never preach again. I remember sitting there feeling horrible for this pastor. Her pastor read a decree against her and gave it to her. She never came back to church. Looking back this was a terrible thing to do, publicly humiliate a pastor. God said touch not my anointed and do my prophets no harm. My God I do not want to be responsible for killing a pastor's spirit. Maybe this pastor was just not ready, I think she should have been given more time. It is one thing to birth a church but, it is a whole other thing to take over a congregation. We have to lead by an example. What is the character of your pastor? Are they always talking about someone? We must be extremely careful of those that tell other peoples business that is never good. Do not ever think that your name is not coming up to someone else in conversation. God is no way pleased with this. He is tired of shepherds' scattering His sheep. This is a serious position to be in, we as pastors have to be very careful that we are not hurting anyone. We should not crush another persons' spirit. Some recover from this and there are many who never recover. When we really truly care for and love the sheep that God sends us He is faithful to send more. If we stay focused on Jesus Christ and continue to lift His name higher and higher, He will gladly draw all men unto Him. God needs willing and yielded vessels to help win souls for Him. He wants no man to be lost. Man can put many demands on ministers and leaders in the church. God said my yoke is easy and my burden is light.

When we get saved, we want our families to get saved. In order for this to happen a smooth transition must take place, it is vitally important to be a part of a loving and healthy church because your family will be drawn to that, people will be drawn to that. There is plenty of work to do in God's vineyard. If it is God leading the ministry, you will have a passion for it, it will give you joy to do. Ministry should not become a burden. This is why it is important to watch the character of the pastor some can be too controlling, demanding and way too hard on people.

Whatever you do must always be done with love, the love of God. God is pleased when souls are won, the angels are singing and rejoicing. We have a lot of work to do and we have to get it right. There are pastors who let their emotions get in the way and they act on them. I have learned that hurt people that have not been healed hurt people this is a profound and true statement. When sheep bite it hurts and sheep will bite, but you as a shepherd should never bite back. God said we will know them by their fruit. If you are in a ministry and fruit is not being produced something is definitely wrong. If the head is right then the whole body would be right. The head causes the body to function. Character means everything. The character of a person will always determine how much fruit you will produce. God is love and we should always extend love to our fellow sisters and brothers and they should always see the love of God in our life. We should recognize our sisters and brothers in Christ. I once preached a message "whose your Daddy." The scripture reading was (John 8:39-47). If you do not recognize another Christian we have to ask ourselves, who are they serving.

I have been taught and trained and some of my teaching was not always correct. God will minister to you on what is right and what is wrong. People can only teach you what they have been taught. Your parents can only parent what they have been taught. Until we give our life to Christ and He begins to minister and correct those crooked places we will become a better parent through Jesus Christ. I would always say, my daughter and my son have two different mothers my daughter grew up with me without Christ and my son grew up with me with Christ in my life. Our focus in life should always be to please God completely and not man. When you seek to please man something is definitely wrong. Your pastor is not your God I'm going to repeat this, your pastor is not your God. Jesus Christ is King of Kings and Lord of Lords. We serve a jealous God so therefore you must be extremely careful who and what you put before God. He wants to be first and foremost in your life and He will take care of everything else. God wants all of His children to be blessed in every area of their lives. Our job as a servant of the most High is to be a good example of Jesus Christ so that our lives will help to win souls for Him. As a pastor when God calls me home I want Him to say come, my child well done good and faithful servant.

Pastors and ministers I strongly encourage each and everyone of you to be extremely careful on how you handle God's children as we all are held accountable for their spirit and soul.

A MESSAGE TO YOU-WINNING SOULS FOR
CHRIST-VICTORIOUS, SUCCESSFUL

"On that day I will gather you together and bring you home again. I will give you a good name a name of destinction, among all the nations of the earth, as i restore your fortunes before their very eyes. I, the Lord, have spoken!" (Zephaniah 3:20 NLT)

God wants us to tell everyone about the goodness of Jesus. Share your testimony on what God is doing in your life. If we lift up the name of Jesus, He will draw all men unto Him. God is looking for those that love His sheep, He said if you love me feed my sheep.

God never wants His sheep to be scattered when sheep are scattered they wander because scatter means to separate and drive to many directions. God is not pleased, this can cause a person to become spiritually confused. It is the shepherds job to protect the sheep from anyone that would scatter them. The bible tells us that Jesus said; "He who is not with me is against me and He who does not gather with me scatters." (Matthew 12:30 NET).

There are many lost souls out in the world to minister to. Jesus said I want no man to be lost. Salvation is given to those that accept Jesus Christ as their Lord and Savior the bible tells us; "If you openly declare that Jesus is lord and believe in your heart that you are made right with God and it is by openly declaring your faith that you are saved." (Romans 10:9 NLT).

"If a man has a hundred sheep and one of them wanders away, what will he do? Won't he leave the ninety-nine others on the hills and go out to search for the one that is lost? And if he finds it, I tell you the truth, he will rejoice over it more than over the ninety-nine that didn't wander away! In the same way, it is not my heavenly Father's will that even one of these little ones should perish." (Matthew 18:12-14 NLT).

You must let your life represent Jesus Christ so that others can see the God in you. Your conduct and character should always line up with the will of God. You must always be transparent and share your testimony with others. When God is blessing someone else, He will bless you. When God is healing someone else, He will heal you. When God is elevating someone else, He can do the same in your life.

CHAPTER 5 – A POISONOUS PERSON

There is such a thing as a poisonous person it could be a mother, a father, teacher or a friend. As parents we have to let our children go so that they can grow. We cannot hold them so tight that we do not give them a chance to experience life for themselves. We are quick to say I do not want you to go through what I have been through. The fact that you are still here to tell the story informs me that you got through it. Experience is always by far the best teacher. This goes for pastors and overseers (apostle's). I believe parents can sometimes do more harm in sheltering their children than nurturing them. This happens to a child that the parent held tight their whole life, never letting them go out and experience life. They became wild when they were let go.

When a pastor is instructed by God to start a church, this is a wonderful thing. They need time to grow individually and with their congregation that God sends them. The apostle should not touch a pastor's sheep. They should never call them, work with them or have anything to do with them. The sheep should know who the apostle (overseer) is, but they should not know them. It is out of order for the overseer to interfere with the sheep. Jesus taught and trained the disciples and sent them out but He did not go with them. You see God will always bring you to different levels through your maturity in Him. Throughout my spiritual journey, I strongly believe that I have reached a level that I was hindered to surpass.

I will provide you with examples of a poisonous person. A mother can be poisonous to her children when she does not know when to stay out of their affairs. When a forty year old man fails to provide for his child and the mother of the child has spoken to him on several occasions about their child's provision with no avail from the father, it is now time to handle this matter legally. A poisonous mother is one that will show up with her forty year old son to every court appearance and will pay for a lawyer to fight the mother of their grandchild for the provision of this child. This mother is sending out such a strong message-- number one she is very controlling, number two I really do not care whether my grandchild has anything and number three by doing so sends a message to the mother by actions, which says I do not care if you have to struggle you are not getting anything. This is a poisonous mother on so many levels. You send out a horrible message to your grown son and this hinders him from growing and standing up to be the father that God intends for him to be. This tells your son that you condone their unacceptable and irresponsible behavior. Your son will never fully mature into manhood when having a poisonous mother such as this and so the grandmother and father walk away going to sleep at night with paying $32 a week which is in no way child support for this child this is absolutely unbelievable! We have to know when to let go or else the individual will never grow into the man that God has created, called, equipped and destined for them to be in life. A father who is teaching his five year old son how to ride a bike with no training wheels is not going to continue to hold the bike as the child rides, at some point father will let go and the son rides his bike on his own. God does the same thing with each and everyone of His children once He sees that we have reached a certain level of maturity.

God is not pleased when we interfere with an individuals growth and maturity as he or she is being processed by Him. An overseer should never hinder the growth and maturity of a pastor. As a pastor, you will feel and know that God is trying to get your attention to be free. There are levels that God needs to get you to in your ministry and this grieves the Holy Spirit and can hinder the anointing and the work that God desires to do in and through His chosen vessels. God said my yoke is easy and my burden is light. This can become a poisonous hindrance to the ministry and can hold up growth. There are overseers that are very controlling, they want to be in charge and too involved in the pastor's ministry. God is not a duplicator. God is an innovator. As much as the overseer tries to duplicate a pastors ministry to be like theirs, every pastor is different and every ministry is different. If you have a poisonous person in your life, it is imperative that you break free from them immediately or you will never reach your full capacity of growth that God has intended for your life. I pray that this chapter will open up the eyes of many that have this kind of controlling person in their life.

You have to know when to let go so that the individual can grow. If you are not sure when to let go ask God, He will show you. We should never hinder another persons growth. God is not pleased with this at all. God will move every hindrance out of the way that interferes with His work. We might say I am waiting for God to do it and God could be waiting for you seek Him. I strongly believe that everyone will see themselves in this chapter whether they may be the poisonous person or they are the one that has someone poisonous in their life.

A MESSAGE TO YOU- A POISONOUS PERSON-TO INFLUENCE WRONGFULLY

Maybe you know someone that may be a poisonous person, maybe you are realizing you are a poisonous person. A poisonous person is constantly interceding and taking control or smothering someone. You can hinder their spiritual growth. God is not pleased, He wants each of us to be made whole, so that we can grow. You have to let go of people and let God. I do not want to be the hindrance to any ones spiritual growth in any capacity. You see, pride always causes one to mistreat others. Pride is always about self and has no regard for others. Pride is behind fights, confusion and slander. Pride can eventually lead to violence when we do not expose it and address it for what it really is. If you feel that you may be a poisonous person, please repent and ask God to show you how to not be poisonous in any ones life or be a hindrance in their spiritual growth. "For all that is in the world- the lust of the flesh, the lust of the eyes, and the pride of life- is not of the Father but is of the world." (1 John 2:16 NKJV).

"Behold, I am sending you out like sheep in; the midst of wolves; be wary and wise as serpents, and be innocent (harmless, guilcless, and without falsity) as doves." (Matthew 10:16 AMP). "Behold! I have given you authority and power trample upon serpents and scorpions, and [physical and mental strength and ability] over all the power that the enemy [posssesses]; and nothing shall in anyway harm you." (Luke 10:19 AMP).

We have to get to a place where we really get to know when satan is in a situation. If it is not lined up with the will of God than it is not of God. Ask God to reveal to you who is for you and who is against you, ask Him to show you who are the poisonous people in your life. So that satan will not outsmart us. For, we are familiar with his evil schemes.

Chapter 6 – Experience is the Best Teacher

Experience is by far always the best teacher. I have learned many lessons of my life from experience. My mother tried to warn me of many things and I refused to hear her. I had to experience it in order to learn from the lesson. People grow through life's exams. How would you know if you can pass the exam if you never studied or been given the test. Every lesson in life that you pass it brings you to another level. Sometimes overseers can get in the way of allowing the pastors to experience things on their own. What you may have gone through and the outcome of that situation may not be the way my situation will turn out. Each one of us have been blessed with gifts and talents. We have gifts that we do not even know exists. I just realized I have a the gift of the scribe to write poems and poetry.

I was trained as a pastor on how to deliver a sermon which is a message from God. I received teaching and training in this area. I never knew that I had this gift in me to preach the gospel of Jesus Christ. I was thrown out there when it was time to open my church and my very first sermon was the day I opened my church. I became very strong in preaching the gospel and grew tremendously because I was let go. Yes, it was the Holy Spirit using me as His chosen vessel. I refuse to take the credit but if I had restraints on me. I would not have reached the levels in this area. I believe hands on experience is the best teacher. Being a correction officer, I was given a new officer to train, while they were on the job training I gave them my keys, my desk and my radio. The only way to really get the full effect of running a unit, I had to let them go to be in charge. I provided excellent training and many new officers thanked me because I let them go and fully run a unit. A teacher that teaches never taught enough because there is so much to be learned. When I grew up there were really no computers and so I had to learn how to use one. If there were a blockage to stop a teacher from continuing their education this could stop their future in teaching. There is always so much to learn because things continue to change daily. The way math was taught to me, they have taken math to another level in its present day teaching.

Experience can be the best teacher because you become wiser and become more skillful in doing it yourself and it qualifies you to get to the next level, as long as there are no hindrances. A person that has been to prison will minister to others on what it is like to be there. This should cause the listener to never do anything to go to prison. Many lessons are taught and learned by experience. We grow so much through the experiences of life. We often test things for our self. Just like a child, if you tell them do not touch something because it is hot, they will often touch it anyway and after doing so the lesson was learned, now they understand the concept of not touching hot things. In ministry, we can take the advice of another pastor or our overseer but the outcome of a situation may not always be like their outcome and every person is different. Our experiences help us to grow as a leader. We will learn from our mistakes and this becomes a test that we have passed and so we grow. We have to allow people to grow and not get in the way of their learning and growing experiences. I remember saying to myself growing up I am going to let my children stay out late and I am not going to be as strict as my parents. Guess what, when I had my own children that did not happen and now I understood why? My parents wanted me in the house early and I find myself doing those things that my parents did with my own children again experience is the absolute best teacher. I did not understand it until I had my own children. Sometimes you just have to let people experience for themselves to become a wise teacher. Many times as we tell our children, not do something they have to go take that exam on their own because they may feel that we do not know what we are talking about. Our best teachers are the elders if we truly listen to them and follow their path we would be so much better off. I am not saying to always experience it for yourself especially when someone is trying to warn you and keep you out of harms way. Seek God in all things in decisions, with your life situations ask Him to show you and He will.

A MESSAGE TO YOU –EXPERIENCE IS THE BEST TEACHER –THE ACT OF LIVING THROUGH AN EVENT, KNOWLEDGE AND SKILL RESULTING FROM THIS.

Life's experience can become our best teacher when we learn from our own mistakes. It can be a lesson well learned. Parents sometimes interfere with life's lessons because we do not want our children to go through what we went through. You have to go through that experience so you can become experienced. You will always learn from your experience.

"As for you, the anointing you received from him remains in you, and you do not need anyone to teach you. But as his anointing teaches you about all things and as that anointing is real, not counterfeit- just as it has taught you, remain in him." (1 John 2:27 NIV).

I learned better by going through a situation than hearing what someone else has gone through. Many times people want to experience it for themselves just because it did not work for you does not mean it will not work for me. You should always share experiences, but do not expect someone to learn from your mistake. We all have to go through hardship and how we get through it each one can tell a different story. Just know that in the midst of what you are going through God said He will never leave you nor forsake you.

CHAPTER 7 – KILL, STEAL AND DESTROY

This is satan's job, he comes to kill your vision, your purpose in life and will do anything to kill your ministry. He is a thief he wants to steal your confidence, your boldness and rob you of your faith. He wants to destroy you so that you will never preach the gospel again. An enemy was sent to my ministry to kill, steal and destroy it. In every bad situation, there is good. During this time in my ministry, I was going through a Job experience. I was losing member after member. My pastor said that God told her to close the doors of her church and He would give her, her own building and she said pastor we will only be with you a little while. Yes, she moved her congregation in with mine. My ministry was finally growing because God sent me wonderful people. They were helping in the ministry and the love was just awesome. When I said we did not have funds to have food for our church anniversary, they got together and cooked. When I moved, they came and helped me. When my pastor and her congregation moved in the people left. My first born evangelist who was the prayer warrior and my armor bearer left. I had only a handful of people left.

The conspiracy began and no one but the Holy Spirit began to show me and tell me what was going on. My overseer, the elder and the leaders began to talk about me and make remarks to say that I was not a good leader, even to the point of convincing me that I am not a good leader and that I am not anointed. I have never met this particular devil before this devil was after my life as a pastor. I did not see this at first because the devil was so cunning. My overseer said pastor you have been doing this a long time now, you need a break. I am going to teach for a few weeks on fasting, giving and praying. This was a set up, she said you sit. The very next Sunday her and her congregation brought in a rug, put up a new banner they moved their things in. I knew my pastor and she was actually sitting me down because remember she is not telling me why I am sitting down but, it appears as though people are not staying in my ministry. I went from people calling my pastor and my pastor calling me saying pastor everyone is calling me saying you are on fire (to God be the Glory) to now I'm sitting down. I was preaching like never before I was on another level. To every level there is another devil. There was a prophet that would come to our ministry and the Holy Spirit told me that she told the overseer to sit me down. I believe the overseer shared with her that I am not a good leader and people are not staying in my ministry. While sitting down, I am now observing everything, and all along the Holy Spirit was showing me that the overseer was trying to take over my ministry. The overseer had a reputation of telling people off from the pulpit. She would make extreme comments that I was not a good leader and I have no anointing without saying my name. The overseer gave me a book called understanding the anointing and this is how I reached another level on my preaching. How did I go from being on fire to no anointing?

I am sitting down every Sunday participating in the service and it looked like I was just a member and not the pastor of the church. I was very obedient to leadership and so I never addressed this with my pastor as to why I was sitting down. I continued to pastor the few people that I had behind the scene. Sitting down, my eyes were beginning to open to all that was going on. The Holy Spirit kept showing me by and by every Sunday I would leave church and cry. God began to minister to me and He showed me that, when my people leave a service they are to be encouraged and not discouraged. They should feel uplifted and not down. They should have joy and peace. I knew that I was never to have anyone leave service like this. God also showed me that all the ministers that left from under the leadership of the overseer felt this pain that I was feeling.

My pastor, the overseer, was not my cheerleader anymore and I could not understand what? and why? was this happening. She put the elder of the church in charge when conducting telephone conferences. I was being treated as though I was not the pastor of the church. I could not even understand what was happening. If you really want to get to know someone let them come live with you. Three months past, and I am still sitting down and I said to my pastor when will I go back to presiding? She said well I want elder to start presiding so that when we leave and go to our own building, she will be able to help me. I am so obedient to authority. If my pastor said sit down, I would sit down, if she said get up, I would get up. I now felt like I was going through a David and Saul experience. Saul saw the anointing on David's life and wanted David dead. Remember an enemy came to my ministry to kill, steal and destroy.

While doing my volunteer work with pastoral care at the hospital in my community, I met an apostle. Her and her husband came to visit my church, after service we spoke and she said she was confused she did not know any one else in the ministry. I know you are the pastor but I did not know who everyone else was. She said pastor sometimes our overseer can be our hindrance and she said you will never treat your ministers the way your pastor treated you. It was a long time before I called this apostle again because, I got very offended when any one talked about my pastor. I continued to sit now for five months, I am still not given a reason as to why I am sitting. My pastor never met with me to talk about it. It is never good to just leave a situation alone and not discuss it and have the person to figure it out on his or her own. A great leader will always address the situation with God's unconditional love and all parties involved. I was beating myself up and I could not figure out what I was doing wrong. All along in my spirit, I kept feeling like my pastor was trying to take over my space and my ministry.

You will always know by the attacks on your life on exactly how big the calling is on your life and just like Job I was tested in many things. This was the first time that I was tested with my ministry. This was a big attack because the enemy had designed this attack so that I would never want to preach or pastor again and that I would just leave the ministry. I thought not only of the few members that where remaining, I thought about all those that are to come. They were counting on me to survive through this. They were counting on me to live and not die. This spoke volumes to me. It confirmed to me that there is a greater call on my life. I was faithful in a few and God was about to give me more. I felt in my spirit that I was about to be elevated into another level.

If satan can stop you from preaching the gospel, than he has won. When you become a willing vessel and decide that you want to do the work that God called and created you to do, God will see you through. God does not remove ministers or pastors that truly love Him and the people that He sends. He said many are called but few are chosen. I thank God I was chosen as this was evident as satan was trying to steal my faith and my anointing. He tried to kill my ministry now and destroy it for the future. All the while I kept giving God praise. I did not look at what I was going through and get upset with God just like Job. I did not understand it, but I did not give up. I just knew this was another test and I shall pass and not fail. People often take their bad situation and instead of looking at the people that satan uses to cause the pain and affliction they get mad at God.

A minister that leaves a church because the church hurt them and they decide they never want to be a pastor again and so they never join another ministry or branch out on their own is a prime example. Satan wants to stop your spiritual growth and he comes to destroy your spirit man. I am here to tell you it was not the church that hurt you it was man that satan used to hurt you. There are so many ministers and people that have gifts and talents that are not using them today because they have been hurt by someone in the church. If you can sing but you were going to church and you were hurt and now you are not singing for the Lord it was satan who stopped you from reaching the masses with your anointed voice. If you are a pastor and you were hurt by your overseer and left a ministry, satan wants to kill the head and he wants to stop you from your destiny and all the souls you would be able to reach for Christ. Now is not the time to give up, in fact your blessing is right there your breakthrough is right there, it is completely up to you to just reach out and grab it.

A MESSAGE TO YOU-KILL, STEAL AND DESTROY-TO TEAR DOWN, DEMOLISH, TO DO AWAY WITH, TO KILL.

Do not let the devil kill your ministry, steal your anointing and destroy your destiny. Remember the devil is a liar and the truth is not in him. If it was left up to the devil he wants no one to preach the gospel. Remember the bible reminds us; "For I can do everything through Christ, who gives me strength." (Philipians 4:13 NLT). "What, then shall we say in response to these things? If God is for us, who can be against us?" (Romans 8:31 NIV).

We have to fight the enemy back and use his tactics to kill his plan of attacks and kill every negative thought and spoken word against your life and your ministry. The more we continue to speak something we bring life to that situation which is the reason the dead bones came alive in Ezekiel is because of the spoken word. "The hand of the Lord was on me, and he brought me out by the Spirit of the Lord and set me in the middle of a valley; it was full of bones.He led me back and forth among them, and i saw a great many bones on the floor of the valley, bones that were very dry. He asked me, Son of man, can these bones live? I said, Soverign Lord, you alone know. Then he said to me prophesy to these bones and say to them, Dry bones hear the word of the Lord!This is what the Sovereign Lord says to these bones; I will make breath enter you and you will come to life. I will make breath enter you and you will come to life I will attach tendons to you and make flesh come upon you and cover you with skin: I will put breath in you, and you will come to life. Then you will know that I am the Lord. So I prophesied as I was commanded. And as I was prophesying, there was a noise a rattling sound, and the bones came together, bone to bone. I looked and tendons and flesh appeared on them and skin covered them, but there was no breath in them. Then he said to me prophesy to the breath; prophesy son of man and say to it this is what the sovereign Lord says: Come, breath, from the four winds and breathe into these slain, that they came to life and stood upon their feet- a vast army." (Ezekiel 37:1-10 NIV).

If you continue to say the doctor said I will not be able to walk after surgery, and you tell other people what the doctor said they will tell others and you can bring life to that negative situation. It begins to have breathe, legs, hands and a body as it comes to life. This is satan's plan to kill God's plan for our lives. Satan wants you to continue to speak the negative report, we will speak positive, claim healing, speak healing, and see healing. Jesus died on the cross for our healing. Satan wants to steal your peace, joy and happiness. He wants to rob you of your faith. We have to know that the enemy comes to attack. Do not stay focused on your current situation. You must pray your way through. The more you pray, the more satan will be defeated. "But He was wounded for our transgressions, He was bruised for our iniquities; The chastisement for our peace was upon Him, And by His Stripes we are healed." (Isaiah 53:5 NKJV).

Satan wants to destroy your destiny so that you do not get all that God has for you. He wants to destroy ministries to stop them from preaching the gospel of Jesus Christ. If he can get a pastor to change their mindset then he has won. There are so many people assigned to a pastor. Do not let the enemy stop you from doing what God called you to do. So many people are counting on you to live and not die. Press your way, God will close doors and open new ones let Jesus lead you all the way. I encourage you to get back to work so your destiny can be fulfilled and your blessings will be bestowed.

CHAPTER 8 – OUT OF ORDER

God is a God of order and everything that He does it is done in decency and in order anything else would be confusion and God is not the author of confusion. Two ministries combining together for three years is out of order. This causes so much confusion in the body of Christ. This is not healthy at all. Two heads will only create a monster. Who is the shepherd if a church has two heads? It is out of order for an overseer to have anything to do with a pastors flock. Overseers are apostles who come to set order not confusion. Apostles help put things in order. Never should an overseer, oversee a pastor publicly, this should be done behind the scenes. When dealing with a pastor who has a congregation this is an office that must be handled differently than any other office. It is out of order for an overseer to come into a pastors house and be disrespectful to the pastor in front of the congregation. God is not pleased with this action. God always does things in decency and in order. This behavior can leave the pastors sheep to not like the overseer because people love and respect their pastor. We must always represent unconditional love and kindness anything else is not of God. I do not dispute that the office of an overseer can be trying because you oversee several ministries. In each ministry, the pastor has a mandate for their own house. God is an innovator not a duplicator. He places special gifts in each pastor and they all have a work to do for the Lord. My ministry is a healing ministry, emotional and physically. When people are physically sick, it is usually due to emotional sickness. When we get emotional healing, we are made whole and the physical body can heal as well. Sickness can take a toll on our bodies. Emotional pain can cause physical pain. We cannot just put a band-aid on our wounds, it must be cleaned and cared for or it can leave an infection within the body. When we are emotionally sick because of hurt, disappointments, loss of loved ones, anything that can cause our hearts to be broken this can put a toll on our health. Often people get angry, become bitter, short tempered, full of pride, this kind of pain can cause our health to deteriorate, if we do not allow God to heal us. Healing comes by sitting under a healing ministry, hearing the word of God, prayer, one on one counsel with your pastor. Being around positive loving people that genuinely want the best for you can put you on your healing road. God wants all of us to be made whole. When we are made whole, this will help to get someone else whole. God loves all of us and He does not want us to be broken. If you have a heavy heart or a broken heart, the only one that can mend it, fix it, is Jesus Christ. He knows your heart better than anyone and He will heal you from any affliction if you just let Him in to help heal you emotionally.

Every ministry is different it is out of order for an overseer to interfere with the office of a pastor and want to change the order of their ministry because it interferes with what God is doing for that house. When an overseer hurts and scatters sheep, this can become a conflict to a pastor who has a healing ministry. This becomes out of order. Pastors become very territorial and will do what it takes to protect their flock. There are many wolves in sheep clothing and they can dress up as leaders in ministry. Anyone that causes separation and division in a ministry is simply out of order. God is a God of Unity. The devil causes confusion in ministries all day, everyday. God wants souls to be won, not scattered. Sheep are not wandering, they are scattered. God is no way pleased and woe to the shepherd that scatters God's sheep. I want to be very careful on how I handle God's sheep and why it is important to keep our flesh and emotions from getting in the way. Confusion can cause us to mistreat and mishandle God's flock. I do not want to be accountable for a person's spirit being broken because I have mishandled them. As pastors, we are held accountable to God for the sheep that He has assigned to our ministry.

It all starts with the head. If the head is not right, then the body will not be right. If the head is hurt, then the people will hurt. The people and the ministers are the body. If the head is out of order, so the body will be out of order. If the head is emotionally whole, then so will the body. If the head is bearing good fruit, then the body would grow healthy and this would make a healthy growing church, anything else would be completely out of order. An overseer, is out of order to ever come in and take over a pastors ministry without probable cause. The basis for probable cause would be with the pastor being out of order causing an embarrassment to God first and foremost and their congregation. When they live a life that totally contradicts Jesus Christ, it has to be a serious problem in the ministry and it should go through the elders and ministry leaders. Again it has to be a probable cause, if not it is out of order.

A MESSAGE TO YOU-OUT OF ORDER- NOT IN PROPER POSITION, FAULTY, BROKEN DOWN NOT IN GOOD CONDITION.

God always does everything in decency and in order. You must always ask God to show you what is out of order in your life and ask Him to put things in His order for your life. Everything satan does is always chaotic and out of order. When I came to Christ, my life was out of order and God began to put things in His order. He removed people that did not mean me any good. What is out of order in your life? What do you need to be put in order? We cannot put things in order on our own and if we could, then we would not need Jesus. We need Jesus Christ to intercede on our behalf at all times. "The Lord says, I will guide you along the best pathway for your life. I will advise you and watch over you." (Psalm 32:8 NLT).

"All scripture is inspired by God and is useful to teach us what is true and to make us realize what is wrong in our lives. It corrects us when we are wrong and teaches us to do what is right. God uses it to prepare and equip his people to do every good work. (2 Timothy 3:16-17 NLT). "Do not be conformed to this world (this age), [fashioned after and adapted to its external, superficial customs], but be transformed (Changed) by the [entire] renewal of your mind [by its new ideals and its new attitude], so that you may prove [for yourselves] what is the good and acceptable and perfect will of God, even the thing which is good and acceptable and perfect [in His sight for you]." (Romans 12:2 AMP).

Chapter 9 – The Restraints

When an overseer sits a pastor down, they are actually spiritually arresting this pastor. You must read this pastor their rights. What are the charges against this pastor? If you have never been told your charges as to why you are sitting down, then you have been illegally convicted. This will cause the Holy Spirit to grieve and you are restraining the anointing without probable cause. When someone is arrested they are read their Miranda rights and they are told the charges that are being brought against them before they go before a judge and a jury to determine whether or not they are guilty. If a person was arrested and not given the Miranda rights or charges this is an illegal arrest. When you spiritually arrest someone, you put them in spiritual bondage. Again you have to have probable cause to sit a pastor down. Example, an elder of the church calls a pastor stupid and that pastor hears it this is probable cause to sit the elder down. I remember going to a service in the poconos and this was such a powerful service and message. The pastor ministered "The restrictions have been lifted." When you are confined and restricted, you are kept within limits? To restrain anyone you control them, you repress them, bind them, hold them back, pin them down and chain them, you are limiting the anointing in them. The opposite of this is freedom to extend and expand. When you are truly free in ministry you allow the Holy spirit to utilize your gifts for the body of Christ. To extend this means to go as far as you can without limits, no limits and your ministry will expand, it will grow to higher heights and deeper depths. When there are no restrictions, the restraints must come off. In the service with the pastor from the poconos, the pastor had a door nailed down to the floor and everyone was given a key to unlock, go through and close the door and lock it on the other side. He said you have a key to the doors so take a deep breathe and embrace the new breathe of life that has been opened unto you and he kept on saying the restraints are off, the restrictions are lifted. I always loved to go to this pastors church. He helps awaken your spirit and you feel refreshed and rejuvenated to continue on in ministry. He gives you a boost to the next phase in ministry.

Every ministry is different, I have to be led by the Holy Spirit in my ministry and not man. God will equip you to finish the work that He called you to do. He equips you to be the pastor that your congregation needs. You cannot put old wine skins into new wine skins. You cannot put a 19 year old ministry with a 9 year old ministry, it will not work. God is not in confusion, we as christians must be extremely careful. God will not put us in spiritual bondage, satan will. Satan wants you to sit that anointing down and shut the mouth of anyone preaching the gospel. Remember he wants to kill your spirit, steal your anointing and destroy your ministry. I told you the greater the attack on your life, the greater the call on your life. Satan wants to destroy anyone that is a threat to his evil kingdom. The devil thought he had me, but I got away.

I had to address the elder of the church because there was a little tension and I confronted her and she said I have a problem with you because you have apostle doing your work. I was shocked now it is all coming out. I said I do not have apostle doing my work. I do not even know why I am sitting down. She said where are all your people at, everyone has left you. I said I am beginning to believe that you may have said something to cause them to leave. I called the apostle and told her what happened. She seemed confused. On that Monday, the Holy Spirit told me there was choir rehearsal today, I called the apostle and said did we have choir rehearsal today she said yes, I said no one called to tell me this, she said pastor you cannot hear me any more you cannot hear me ever since elder said what she said you cannot hear me. Lord Jesus, she was absolutely right. I cannot hear her anymore, I can now hear the Lord speaking to directly to me.

I called the overseer and I took back my ministry that the devil tried to steal from me. I told her that she began to oversee me publicly and not behind the scenes. She would usurp my authority in front of my congregation because I let her. I told her that I was always taught that two heads make a monster, having two congregations together is never good and is simply out of order. She began to get sarcastic with me as I was talking saying Aah! Ooh! Aah! Ooh! She said oh! so now I am the reason you do not have any people in your church. I did not say that she did. She said well how can I fix this since I made a mess of this. I told her I was going back to presiding and I will no longer sit down. I took the church back. She said, my pastors appreciation dinner is coming up and I want elder to preside over it. The Holy Spirit continued to minister to me and showed me that I was never to put the elder on my pulpit again. The devil thought he had me but I got away and I broke free from the shackles and just like Paul and Silas did. I continued to pray, seek the face of God and give God praise until this day the chains fell from off of me completely.

A MESSAGE TO YOU- THE RESTRAINTS - TO HOLD BACK FROM ACTION, CONFINEMENT AND SILENCE.

Do not ever let anyone wrongfully restrain you in ministry if you are feeling some type away in your spirit, then something is not right. The Holy Spirit will never steer you wrong. You must always go with that feeling in your gut and spirit to break loose from that bondage. The opposite to restraints would be freedom and liberty, this sounds like the Holy Spirit so any other way must be satan. Satan wants you to be in bondage on a permanent basis. He wants to put shackles on you and over your mouth from preaching the gospel. He is a liar, he comes to wrongfully accuse you, arrest and lie on you. We have to be like Paul and Silas, they prayed until the shackles fell off of them and the jail gate was opened. Why? Because, prayer always changes everything. Satan wants to stop your praise. If you stay focused on your situation, it will always cause doubt to creep in, your praise to stop, you will not want to pray and unbelief sets in. These are your weapons to fight with, you need your faith so that you can see those things that are not, as though it were.

Please know that when the praises go up the blessings will always come down. Your praises can shake heaven and earth. Your prayer will always change things. We must always pray without ceasing. We have to trust God in all things trust Him even when it looks like there is no way out. He will deliver you from the enemy's hands. Hold on, help is on the way. God loves you and He does not want you in bondage. "He will free your mind, your spirit, your heart, your gifts and when Jesus Christ frees you, you are free indeed. If the Son sets you free, you are truly free." (John 8:36 NLT).

CHAPTER 10 – A HOUSE DIVIDED FALLS

I am back on my post presiding over service. The Holy Spirit ministered to us and showed us that God is love. I received the rolling of eyes from the overseer and the elder. I continued on with the service. The overseer told me not to call her people to help in the service that I was to only use my people. A house divided will surely fall. When we are worshiping together, under the same roof everyone should help in the ministry. You stop the other ministers from using their gifts. The house of God will operate in its fullness when every body part is moving. A little bit of division can cause a house to fall down. Example, you let your sister and her family come to live with you and they do not want to help cook or clean the house because, it is not their house. Everyone must do their fair share. This is too much confusion, this is why it should never be two ministry's together. Satan does not like unity, he wants division and this is division. All it takes is just a little bit of division to enter in and now the house that was built on a rock will fall down. You give satan legal access to destroy a house. Satan loves to cause division. He will cause division in a marriage, he does not like when two become one and he will try all kinds of tricks and schemes to break apart what God has joined together. A house divided will fall it takes everyone in the household to come together to keep it standing. If you are not paying close attention satan will try to destroy any household especially a household of faith. You have to see the tricks of the enemy.

Example, a family friend can go behind your back and tell your family member things that you would not want them to know about, you find out about it through someone else why?

You find out because satan always gets exposed You can handle this by confronting that family friend or confronting the family member. I say do not touch this at all as this is satan trying to cause confusion in your family and trying to divide it. You have to pay close attention and you will see the enemy sneaking up. You do not have to address everything. When you do not expose it, confront it and address it, then you have fully given it over to

God. You put this in the right hands now because God will turn this around in your favor. I am beginning to see satan more and more and I continue to shut him down and stop the enemy in his tracks. Satan would love to cause confusion in any household. He tries to destroy the head of the household which is the husband or pastor. He wants him out of the house remember he hates unity, he hates when people are on one accord, he hates when we are gathered together in Jesus name and he hates a family that prays together. Prayer can destroy satan's tricks. Continue to stay prayerful, satan hates a prayer warrior and will try anything to distract you from your prayer life you have to continue to (P-U-S-H) pray until something happens.

The more you give God praise, the more the blessings will surely flow down. When you were a child you always had that one friend that was a trouble maker, she would tell your friends lies about you just to get them to not be your friend. Why? because, satan hates unity. When everyone is getting along he tries to come in and destroy that. If we go through our spiritual journey with keeping this in the forefront of our mind that satan wants to divide and separate, we would be alright and we will see him in every negative situation. God is love and we should be love too. If we are not operating out of love, then we are not operating in the spirit, we are operating out of our flesh. Our flesh must die daily. We do not have time to entertain the devil. He wants front row seat of confusion, division and separation. Instead give him front row seat of unity, order and one accord. The church that operates out of division eventually will fall. God wants our houses in order, we have to get it right. You must stay away from people that like to cause division. They cannot stand when people are getting along and happy satan will use them to break this apart. Do not let your house be divided it will fall.

A MESSAGE TO YOU-A HOUSE DIVIDED FALLS-TO MAKE OR KEEP SEPARATE AND TO CAUSE TO DISAGREE.

Satan hates unity. Satan comes to separate, he wants to divide families, relationships and marriages. Whenever something is divided eventually it falls. You have to know when satan is trying to cause division in your life. Stay focused and you will see when Satan is trying to cause division when you see it, shut him down immediately. How do you shut him down?

You should never let division get into the situation. You should never give into the plan of the enemy. He will try his best to destroy a marriage. He hates when two are made one, a marriage couple does not even know the kind of power that they have over satan. Satan wants to get the head out of the household. This can do damage to any family. We have to see his tricks and stop satan in his tracks.

You have double the power the bible tells us; "For where two or three are gathered together in my name, I am there in the midst of them."(Matthew 18:20 NKJV).

In every bad situation satan is creeping his way in. God will turn it around for your good purpose just as He did for Joseph. "But as for you, you meant evil against me; but God meant it for good, in order to bring it about as it is this day, to save many people alive." (Genesis 50:20 NKJV).

Trust God in all things, God wants unity the opposite of divide is to unite, combine and connect. Jesus wants us to build our house on a rock so that when satan comes it will not fall down. "Therefore whoever hears these sayings of Mine, and does them, I will liken him to a wise man who built his house on the rock; and the rain descended, the floods came, and the winds blew and beat on that house; and it did not fall, for it was founded on the rock. But everyone who hears these sayings of Mine, and does not do them, will be like a foolish man who built this house on the sand: and the rain descended, the floods came, and the winds blew and beat on that house; and it fell. And great was its fall." (Matthew 7:24-27 NKJV).

Chapter 11 – God is Love

If there is no real love in a ministry, I mean really loving the people and helping them genuinely, then it will not last. God is love and He does all things out of love. God knows our hearts. He searches our hearts and sometimes He finds greed and jealousy. Do not let these vices fill your heart. God would not want your spirit to get broken and crushed. He wants every man to be saved. God will not lead a pastor or overseer to kill a person's spiritual walk with Him. God gathers, He does not scatter. I have heard pastors say God told me to do this. God told you to hurt a pastors heart to humiliate them publicly, that they would not ever want to pastor again. God told you to ignore the people so they can leave your congregation. God told you to tell a minister off and hurt their heart. We have to be very careful. God is love and you will know it is God because it will be done with love and kindness, and in decency and order. When you do not want the people that God has sent into your ministry, how can the Lord send you more people.

Everyone is precious to God. Remember God loves the sinner. He hates the sin. You have no right to cause someone such heartache that they would never go into a church or trust a pastor again. God is love and in order for us to love each other the love of God must be in us. How could we say we love God, but we do not love others? God will chastise us with love and kindness. When God does something a person will receive it. When man does it, it will crush the persons spiritual walk. The closer you get to God the better off your life will be. He will set you up for good things. He will change a stony heart into a heart of compassion. When God has a call on your life, it is always to help win souls for Him so that no man would be lost. God wants to bless your life so that you can be a blessing to others.

You must remember to stay away from poisonous people that can hinder your walk with God. Poisonous people are controlling and want to control your life, when God wants to control it. God wants us to surrender our life to Him and free us from people and things that can keep us in bondage. You will find that your life experiences are your best teacher.

When you are going through something there is a lesson to be learned and God will show you the lesson, just ask Him. Always keep in mind with every level there is another devil that is trying everything to kill, steal and destroy you spiritually. Please stay focused on the prize which is Jesus Christ. He said no weapon formed against you shall prosper. Ask God to show you what is out of order in your life and then watch Him put all things in order for you. He loves us and wants our lives in order. God does not put us in restraints. He wants us to be free indeed.

If God put us in restraints, then He would stop us from making bad decisions and wrong choices. He gave us complete freedom to do as we please. Without God in our lives, we tend to make bad decisions and wrong choices. With God in your life, there are no limits as to what He can do in and through you. God does not want any of His children in bondage. He gave his only son so that we can be free from bondage. There is power in the name of Jesus to break every chain of bondage. Any time there is division, there will be separation if a house is divided it will fall. Satan hates unity and will try everything possible to tear apart. Know that whatever door that God closes for you He will open up a greater door. I have seen Him do it. He is a God that will increase and not decrease. When you truly experience God's love, He will release you into greater things, things you have never seen or experienced. Through Christ we can do all things. God's love will keep us. He will protect you.

God will guide you and direct you, provide for you, work out every obstacle, restore you, give you peace, joy and happiness, and set you up for greatness. You will make wise decisions, you will have great victories, and you will have a friend, a father and mother. Expect a good life, expect blessings to increase and multiply, become better parents, better wives and husbands, and He will show favor over your life, and give you strength, heal you, mend your broken heart, increase your faith like never before, give you double for your trouble. You will learn much, discover hidden gifts and talents, you will never be alone. He makes your crooked path straight, comforts you when needed, loves you unconditionally, and loves a sinner. This is a list of a few things that God can do in your life, when you surrender and give your life to Him. I am extremely glad that I did surrender my will to God and I have seen Him do all these things and more in my life.

A MESSAGE TO YOU-GOD IS LOVE-A STRONG AFFECTION OR LIKING FOR SOMEONE, CARE FOR AND TO HOLD DEAR.

God is love. "But anyone who does not love does not know God, for God is love." (1 John 4:8 NLT). "No, despite all these things, overwhelming victory is ours through Christ, who loved us. And I am convinced that nothing can ever separate us from God's love. Neither death nor life, neither angels nor demons, neither our fears for today nor our worries about tomorrow- not even the powers of hell can separate us from God's love." (Romans 8:37-39 NLT).

"For God so loved the world that He gave his one and only Son, that whoever believes in him shall not perish but have eternal life." (John 3:16 NIV).

"This is how God showed his love among us; He sent his one and only Son into the world that we might live through him. This is love: not that we loved God, but that he loved us and sent his Son as an atoning sacrifice for our sins. Dear friend, since God so loved us,we also ought to love one another." (1 John 4:9-11 NIV).

"Dear friends, let us continue to love one another, for love comes from God. Anyone who loves is a child of God and knows God. But anyone who does not love does not know God, for God is love." (1 John 4:7-8 NLT).

"For I know the plans I have for you, "says the Lord." "They are plans for good and not for disaster, to give you a future and a hope." (Jeremiah 29:11 NLT).

"Give thanks to the God of heaven. His faithful love endures forever." (Psalms 136:26 NLT).

Chapter 12 – The Release

When God wants you to be released, you will be released. When you have been freed by the Lord you are free indeed. The hardest thing I ever had to do was to call my pastor the overseer to say I bless God for you and all your teaching and training. God is releasing me from under your leadership. He is leading me in a new direction after I hung up the phone a peace came over me and that nervous feeling was gone and I knew that God released me to do other works. My assignment was up in this ministry and my pastors' assignment with me was up. This is the time for me to lean and depend on Jesus even more. I have to trust Him even in this. While writing this book there where attacks because satan does not want me to finish this book because many will read it and get back to ministry and many will get back into a church to have a covering and many will be convicted and delivered. To God be the glory, often times in life we are waiting for God and God is waiting for you.

When God has delivered me from situations He shows me each time He was speaking directly to me. God does not set you free from a ministry for you to now do nothing especially when there is so much more work to be done. You must continue the work until your season is just up and God is now bringing you into another season. Please know that God has a divine plan for your life and some of us give up because we feel like we cannot make it. We can do all things through Christ who has strengthened us. When you are weak, than God is made strong.

Satan will always try to interfere with your walk with Christ upon being released. All along I kept feeling that the overseer was trying to take over my church space and it was confirmed by God. Two days later after I was released, she went to the director of the facility where I had church space, she told her that she was the CEO of the church and I was no longer in her ministry and she would take over the space. I was given a call by someone and they informed me of what she was doing. I immediately called the director and I explained to her that I have been trying to get a hold of her and I left several messages as, to explain this confusion. I told the director that the space was given to me in 2004 and just because I am no longer under the overseers ministry that does not prohibit me from starting my own. I am not in a binding contract with the overseer. This confirmed on what I was feeling all along. A house divided fell. The director decided to not give the space to either of us I believe she did not want to get involved.

GOD CLOSED THE DOOR, AND HE WILL OPEN BETTER DOORS TO MY NEW BEGINNINGS.

There were many restraints from being in this facility and when He released me I instantly became free from all bondage. I know the next building that God gives me there will be no **RESTRAINTS.** God will increase not decrease. To God be the Glory! If you are in spiritual bondage or in a relationship or a situation that you need to be free from ask God to help you, to give you strength to break free. Remember, we can do all things through Christ that strengthens us. I am continuing to move forward in my new ministry.

Yes, this might have been a horrible experience, but I am not focusing on what happened, I am focusing on what I am to do now. God called me to do a work and it will get done. I thank God that I was able to see that my journey's in my life was a pathway to my future. I know that God has a greater future for me and that is why? as I was traveling down that journey there were many obstacles in the way to stop me from reaching my gifts and destiny. As I look back over my life and everything that I went through was just a distraction and a hindrance only to slow me up from getting there. My blessings might have been a little delayed but they are not denied. To God be the Glory! Get up and pick up your cross and follow Jesus. He is waiting on you. I pray that every reader would be released and set free from any bondage whether it is in your mind, spiritual bondage, relationship or anything that is causing you to feel bound. There will be many struggles along the way to your destiny but the key is that you must stay close to Jesus Christ and He will always see you through. So many people are counting on you to survive. Stay focused and you will meet up with your destiny at the appropriate time.

A MESSAGE TO YOU-THE RELEASE-TO LET GO, A RELEASING FROM A PRISON, FREEDOM, LIBERATION AND DELIVERANCE.

"You have allowed me to suffer much hardship, but you will restore me to life again. And lift me up from the depths of the earth." (Psalms 71:20 NLT).

"Now may the Lord of peace himself give you his peace at all times and in every situation. The Lord be with you all." (2 Thessalonians 3:16 NLT).

"In that day the Lord will end the bondage of His people. He will break the yoke of slavery and lift it from their shoulders." (Isaiah 10:27 NLT). I want to encourage you today your day is coming.

"What's more, I am with you, and I will protect you wherever you go. One day I will bring you back to this land. I will not leave you until I have finished giving you everything I have promised you." (Genesis 28:15 NLT).

"Now may our Lord Jesus Christ Himself and God our Father, who loved us and gave us everlasting consolation and encouragement and well- founded hope through [His] grace (unmerited favor), Comfort and encourage your hearts and strengthen them [make them steadfast and keep them unswerving] in every good work and word." (2 Thessalonians 2:16-17 AMP).

I AM LIVING MY LIFE ON PURPOSE BECAUSE GOD HAS A PURPOSE FOR MY LIFE. I BIND BACKLASH IN THE NAME OF JESUS CHRIST. I BIND ALL CURSES THAT HAVE BEEN SPOKEN AGAINST ME. I BLESS THOSE WHO CURSE ME, AND PRAY BLESSINGS UPON THOSE WHO DESPITEFULLY USE ME. I BIND ALL SPOKEN JUDGEMENT MADE AGAINST ME, AND JUDGEMENTS I HAVE MADE AGAINST OTHERS, AND I BIND AND RENDER USELESS ALL PRAYERS NOT INSPIRED BY THE HOLY SPIRIT, WHETHER PSYCHIC, SOUL, FORCE, WITCHCRAFT OF COUNTERFEIT TONGUES THAT HAVE BEEN PRAYED AGAINST ME, MY FAMILY, AND MINISTRY IN THE NAME OF JESUS CHRIST AMEN, AMEN, AND AMEN.

GRACE AND PEACE TO ALL!

About the Author

I have been pastoring for ten years now. I was led by the Holy Spirit to write this book to help those who gave up ministry or stopped attending church. God has so much for you and wants to bring you to higher heights and deeper depths, but the enemy will fight you in every way to prevent you from reaching a higher spiritual level.

I'm here to tell you life goes on and ministry continues. I am continuing to do the work God has equipped me to do. The devil thought he had me, but I got away. I'm standing stronger and persevering longer. Please, I urge you, get back to work, pick up your cross, and follow Jesus. Watch Him move in your life like never before. Grace and peace be with you!

To contact the author Pastor Denise L. Wade
Email address is: Letmegosoicangrow@gmail.com

Printed in the United States
By Bookmasters